The Wayfaring Strangers

Shrshtee Choudhary

Clever Fox
PUBLISHING

CLEVER FOX PUBLISHING
Chennai, India

Published by CLEVER FOX PUBLISHING 2022
Copyright © Shrshtee Choudhary 2022
All Rights Reserved.

ISBN: 978-93-90850-37-2

Humans are perhaps the strangest creatures
to have ever walked this earth,
to have ever delved into the oceanic depths or
even to have ever left searching for the stars,
Though times have changed
we still set out to explore the ocean,
the black skies vast and limitless potentilal
of granting us knowledge and meaning.

roaming
Forever seeking more from life,
And in this time we have discovered.
The hand paintings by cave men,
litratures lost over the ages,
Music, art, each a beauty incompatible in exiestance
amoung ourselves.... And In all these ventures, we
have learned. Hoarding knowledge in massive heaps
of accumilations, like a bear before the first snowfall,
collecting and collecting for the sake of those who come
after us, in rememberance of those who came before us;
our forefathers', our foremothers'.
And we still tread these waters today, paddling our
little boats, our little canoos over the grandiose and
magnificiant questions of exiestance to where the rivers
of truth and of desire merges into the ocean of life.
in search of ourselves, in search of meaning,
in search of more.........
but the galaxy's, the land and these oceans,
the journeys that we take over these uncharted waters,
are ethreal and yet dangerous. the storming waves of the
ocean are not gentle.The ocean stands a beast only as
beautiful as it is unforgiving.........endless...
boundless, but it has known life.
It is life, in all its chaotic glory, in its essence it is life.

In the darkest, coldest depths of the ocean
that words could not describe;
life still grows and it blooms and celebrates
the joys of existence, dances in love and bathes in a
fruitful life lived...... and then it perishes.
Just like that all life ends,
Not with the same blaze of glory is has lived in
but in a meek and forgettable manner,
here for a second and then suddenly not.
But what stays is an echo of who we are,
who we once were, an endless scream of 'I was here'
in everplace we once inhabited, in everyplace we once
called our own and even in the very soil we may rest in,
our souls like those who came before us will rest in them
after we are gone.
Death knows nothing of time nor of life
but it knows love and kindness and even peace.
I am here as I was here and I will be here forevermore,
even when my heart no longer beats, when you have
forgotten every last memory of me, know that I rest in
the solemn trees, the flowers, the bees,
these pages and even in your bones.

So if you ask me the question of who I dedicate this to.......
I will dedicate this to love, I dedicate this to grief, to
memory, to my flesh and blood my family who shaped
me into the person I stand as today and I dedicate this to
every person who needed these simple words like a soft
blanket on a stormy winter night.
Here is to all the wayfaring strangers lost on their
journeys, with the hope you may find some kind of shelter
within these pages.
With all my love and my deepest of sorrows,
I hope you find comfort here.

Shrshtee Choudhary.

Mother

Mother, would you be proud of me?
If I let my tears seep into ink I use for poetry

Mother, I hope you can forgive me
I may let their words they say underneath my skin
But I do let it fall off my lips like a euphony,

I am a poet you say?
With a way with words and a crave to be heard
But mother, my writings are simply of what I see.

Heart Of Glass

Oh my dear starling
Oh my dear doe,
Sometimes when we say love
We really just mean hope,

So please be cautions
of the flames that you stroke,
a heart of glass
is tough to mend
once it has truly broke.

Me

If younger me
could see me now,
I'd tell her

I swear it gets better,
The world is so much bigger
than this one town

I know you fell drowned out,
I know you feel dragged down

But you were never alone
Back then
And your still not now,

And its for the best that we both
figured that out.

Paper house

Loving someone could be so strange
How quickly we go
From love to hate

But the lies are so much sweeter
When they come from you oh!
Paper house,

Where no one cares and she's alone
Where you forget coming home

So she wastes her time
painting paper flowers
At this hour
Inside this paper house,

Where love is a mockery
Of a shadow

And we're just two paper figures
Living like strangers
Inside one burning house.

Where we feign the world is fine
But oh! Do beautiful things
Still exist?
Inside of fires,

Oh! Why must you cling to this paper town?

This paper house and paper cars
And paper dolls and broken heart's
Living all together,
Is it so better?
In paper towns.

Apollo's daughter

Patience and virtue,
Are things I learned from you,

Midas' touch may turn
Life to gold
But all fades in front of
The vibrancy
Of your soul,

If the sun were to ever laugh
Father I know he would sound
just like you,

Icarus flew too close
When he really should have known
A pedestal that high
Is only
Your own,

Father the only man I ever love
could only ever be you.

Your beauty, its blinding.

Glowing with the light and life of a thousand suns
is not delicate,
there is sheer beauty and power
in ever colour you radiate

with the shine of your eyes
the other worldly nature of your heart
bleeding me out, poision leaving at you touch

I think I know love better now
With the sight of you before my eyes
Sight of someone
civilization would have started wars over.

The shape of your smile, the sound of your laugh
The thought of it fading could truly break me in half

I wish between these pages I could describe you better
But the best I can do for the sake of the readers-Know,
Anything anyones ever loved in me I got them from her

I am a mimicry of your existence,
I am your reflection, almost a splitting image
So take my body, take my soul, take my everything
Its your's
First bounded by blood and now bounded by these words,
For you, my sister I would ruin this whole damned world.

As long as you're alright,
They can burn.

Struck by the bow

I'm a lost traveller
In search of my home,
The trees, they sing me a balled
A story we all know

A story of an archer
Who fell in love
with a doe,

the story they tell me
it pierced my very soul

one autumn, few years
or perhaps it was eons ago?
When a wayfaring stranger
Had wandered down
this same very road,

the archer, he swore,
to never hunt,
forevermore.

The doe's woeful eyes
Had broken the cube of ice
That surrounded the archers heart

But their fate was set in stone,

In another idyllic world
The doe would never leave
And the archer would have never
Picked the bow,

But alas, the doe does die
Tears brim around the archers eyes

And the world moves on.

Burn gold

I've come too far
to watch the sun
burn the sky

a vivid shade of gold

from the top of this
fragile paradise

when the light dimmers'
and it dies
and it dies,

we fear we won't make it
past the night,

but don't worry dear,
new beginnings start
at the endings

and our new path
shall be lit by the stars themselves.

I would know

(inspired by song of Achilles)

I would know him by voice alone,

I would know him
Even if the stars are all gone,

I would know him
With my eyes closed,

I would know him by his soul,

I would know him,
even at the end of the world.

Hopeless elixers

Remember when we drove,
Two whole hours on the road
All the way out
To the nearest country town

For nothing more than starsight
We just gazed up at the sky

We were hopeless from the start
Should have known
When love doesn't last,

Like even time had, slowed down for us
To figure out, what we want

But we just stared up at the sky,
Sitting underneath
The yellow campers light

And even if all the stars were to align
How can you save love that's already died?

Might as well, borrow my matches.

Fire is fire,
It burns just the same
You never know when a spark
Can turn into a flame.

What can turn my heart into ash
Can set your world ablaze,

Burn like the aftertaste of old memories
You wished to never see again.

Fire is fire,
And it will burn
You as well as I

In this pandemonium of silence
In this house we call our home.

But I swear to you,
Never again.

Time

Time
Means nothing
Anymore,

When you wait for the ocean
To hit the shore,

Something out of a fable
Or a lore

Comes to me
A story untold

Or maybe another iteration
Of one we already know?

How would you know?
At the edge of the world

Time,
Means nothing
Anymore.

This lane

I knew dreams come true
The day I met you,
Got no plans
And nowhere left to go,

Maybe we can learn to live,
Only us together

Maybe we could know better,
Even if we never,
make it too far

we can always end this tale
With the last words saying

We lived forever
In our own little dream world,

Maybe we could leave together,
Go somewhere far away

Maybe we could find
someplace better,
maybe all we need
Is a little courage in us
To drive down this lane.

Saprophyte

Let me roam through the wilderness,
Through the darkest side of the woods

Where no light has ever shown

And there would still be
More life there,

Flourishing
In its depth,

Than you have ever known.

Father

The moon shines its brightest
At the darkest of nights,

The heart is versatile in its nature
Think I've seen its many sides,

I have known you,
Have known the kind of love
That keeps one alive.

The honeycomb eyes,
The tea past midnight

No time could tell,
No words could ever spell,
The story of all I love about you,

And forever may seem to stretch
A very long time
But with you on my side,

Father
I know I have found
The kind of love that never dies.

Glow

Your eyes
Can outshine
Every star in the universe
Brighter than any light

Brighter than anything I have ever known,

Leading me out the dark
Saving my very soul,

Could I be dreaming?

Wicked games

The fair snow falls
As the winter winds blow,

The lone wolf,
She still dies alone.

The pack was wise
They at night,
They came in strides,

My little wolf chose to hide away.....

Bit her neck, tore her down
Hunters and prey
These are wicked games
Even angles play

My little wolf chose to run!
Run far away!

Sights hurled past
Underneath one tree
The devil sat
She might have thought
She'd outrun them at last,

But 'the innocents are always prayed'
Even he pitifully gazed,

Searching for a hide out, searching for another chance

She begged to any luck
She might have had,

But they rounded the corner
her prospect turned
black,

and too late its gone
it won't ever come back.

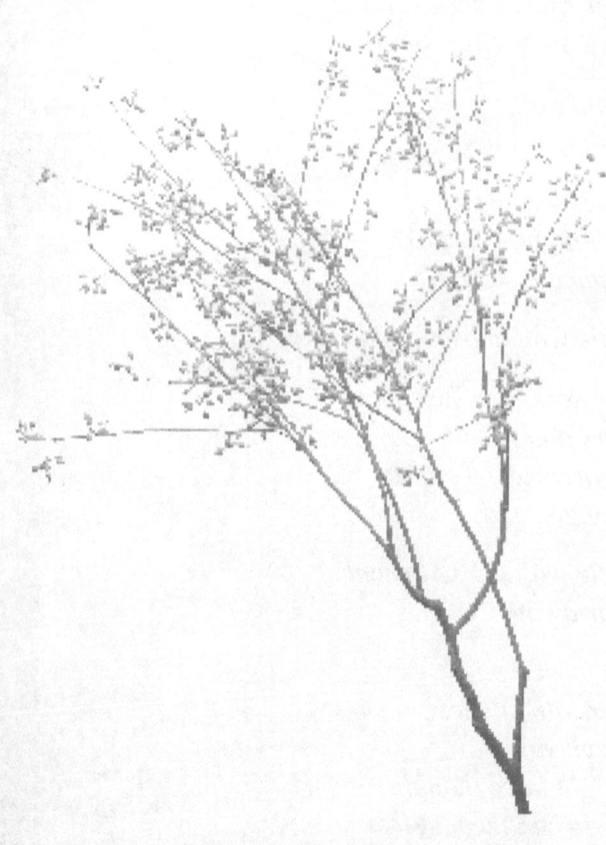

A warring species

young belligerent
lover of war,
hear the trumpet's
the sound of war.

your sins be paid
with your head on a salver,
for with every drop of blood
they cried me river.

Bitter fruit of solitude

Bitter is the fruit,
I cherished it with my anger

I fed it till it bloom,
My fruit of solitude
Its extract bleeds my ire,

I watered it with my pain,
Till the tree outgrew my envy
But it kept on growing higher

Still sweeter than my blood
I still ate it with desire,

Before you can know love, understand pain,
It's a process,

And we all drown in this mire.

As it is

In all my time
All I've ever know

There is one thing
And only one thing alone

That ever drives people
And that thing is control.

A bed of grass

When I shed my armor,
When I shed my pride,
Will you lay my body down underneath
The stary night sky

Bury me near a river and a forest wild
For when the reaper comes I shall go with a smile,

Bury me underneath an orchid
Or with daisies white

It has been what a long time traveling, my dear,
Traveling alone,
With only you by my side,
And all just to lay this body down.

Now rest in this bed of grass
With the sweet melancholy song of our past,
Rest my soul
Once they lay this body down

This shell is nothing more
than a vessel to outgrow,
I hope you find love somewhere else
After you burry me down
The time has come to say our last goodbyes,

So farewell my dear! Don't cry,

Please no sorrow in the last song we share,
As you lay this body down

Farewell my love for now is the time to go
It has been such a long time travelling this road

Traveling and traveling and
All just to lay this body down.

Ego

Down on my ego
Like sipping on a glass of wine,

Hiding in this labyrinth
Choking on my pride,

its hard to change some endings
Othello gets blinded
by his own envy

'nothing more we can do' she argues back

So she lays here wasting her potential
Trying to outrun
Whats the most essential.

Living in the dreamscapes
Of the world she lives in fear

My dear,
The pen of fate is in your hands
But if you never put the quill to page
I don't know
If we will ever make it out the neverlands

Peace in me

Death must be beautiful
What its like to rest in serenity
To bathe in the silence of solemn trees,
To taste the sweet apple of harmony

Take my hand darling
Gently,
Wrap me in an embrace
And show me what it means,
To forget of time
Forgive this life,
To finally know what is peace.

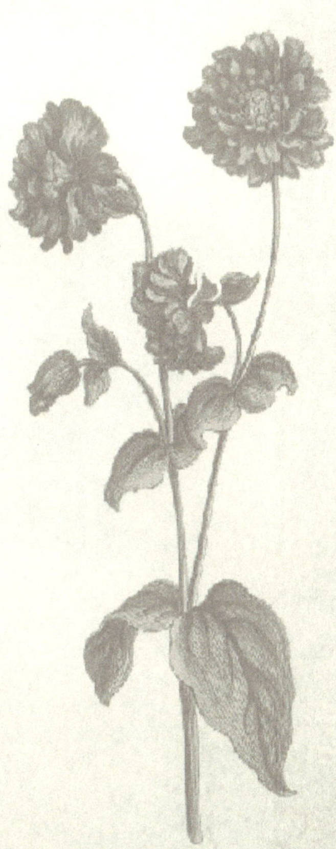

Forever, even after we are gone

Sweet death, kind death,
you don't understand why
my love stays here and grows day and night?

For me? It is a long time
Before I have to say my last goodbyes,
But my soul may mellow here
Forever and ever
In this realm,
Benign.

Ocean falls

The gentle waves of ocean
Rise and fall
And still show me the start and end
Of everything beautiful.

Though this body may succumb to dust
It would only be just,
If my heart stays here
Undying and eternal.

Kills me slowly

'Oh! my Sweet siren,
Sing my serene song
Your voice is enticing
I'm a captive to the sound.'

Your melody,
it consoles me,
I beg of you
Grant me,
this mercy
And sing this little song.....

A soft ending is all my heart longs,

To fall gently
As the curtains
Are finally
Drawn.

Burnt letter

Sometimes bad things happen
And there's little we can do,
I've been so sick of crying
So what I'm going to do
Is say sorry
To you,
I'm sorry
To me,
I'm sorry to us
And for what we have been through,

Just so you know,
That I loved you.

My lanterns

Some stories end at new starting's,
With the fall of the curtains
Enveloped in darkness

When the lights go out
And our tale meets its end
Don't you worry dear,

We can walk the last few steps
Together through the night,
With some lanterns.

A blue whale, wanders

Wandering through the depth
Of the deep blue sea
I search for treasures
In the abyss
Dark and haunting.

Searching for broken pieces
Of forgotten poetry
hints of philosophic reveries,

Or just a verse that is timeless

To add to my collection of beautiful
Objet d'arts
objects I hoard
And name rarities'.

The beast in me

From the darkest abyss
Of the deepest ocean
I hear something call out to me

Calling my name,
Like a hunter at play
And what calls out should terrify me

I have realised my own self
To be
My worst enemy

And the realisation itself
Half conquered the beast.

Mortifs of a shipwreck

The house stood
At the edge of the coast,
Empty
And free of everything

With creaking floors
And an old oak door

An ambient macabre
Fell like a curtain
Over these desolated halls

Right where you left me
Forgotten like just another memory

Never had I ever known a night so long
Than the night in our home
Without you

Never should have ever
Opened my doors
When you stood
Nothing more
Than a shipwreck
All over my shore

You said you never meant
To gamble with our fate

But you seem more and more
Like a stranger
As of late

And our house stood
At the edge of the coast
Now empty
And free of everything...

And I was free too.

To my sister, my blood oath

I'll be your blood
I'll be your home
In this life
And all the next to come

You're my shadow
You're my reflection
The only place I belong

In the air I breath
Inside my very soul

A spell as well
May this be my oath

Extending to eternity
And
Forever and evermore.

Dead man dancing

The laugh of sorrow
Every sound echos hollow

Dancing
In the night
At the gallow

Dancing
To make this pain
Somehow mellow

Made some mistakes
In the past
But now he ain't got no shot
At tryna be a better fellow.

And now he's just a dead man dancing.

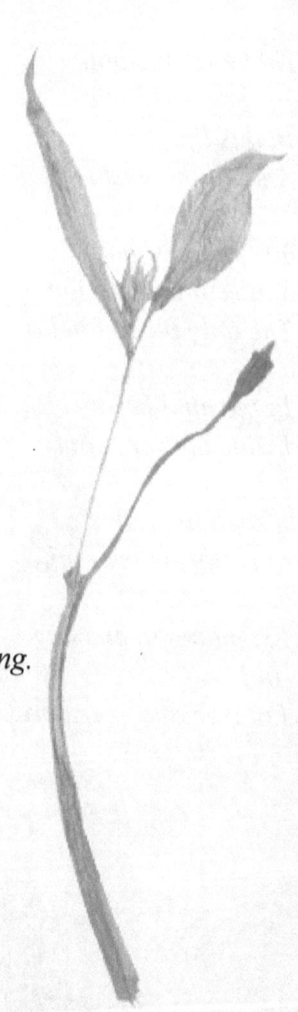

Blessed be

Blessed be the man
That knows both peace and war
For only he truly knows what lies in store,

Blessed be the heart
That stayed kind till the end
The mother that rocked me to sleep
And told me all wounds would mend

Blessed be all those
Who called me their home
When I strayed too far away
When my eyes turned to stone

Blessed be the girl
Who shouldered more pain than her own
Calmly reaping all the love she had sown

Blessed be the child
Naïve heart often lies
But kindred be all those who try and try and try.

Master of illusion

White lies woven by weeping stars
So intricately
By a master of his craft

Woven into the fabric of his being
Was a silver tongue
Like you've never seen

Such needles of decite
That wove him into being

Every bit of the devil
He's even seemed,
Once you've lived at the recivers end
Of one of his schemes.

Final celebration's

When rotten is a soul
A blackned heart it finally holds?

If youre lungs all burn to coal
If the flames, they surround your home

Than raise your glass
And sing along

For if we are to burn
Shan't we all burn together?

My unspoken truth

Take my hand
As you have taken my life too
For I have at last
Found a home inside you

And I hope you know
That it means
Forevermore

With every word I bleed
Into this ink
Along my tears too

Know that my heart stays true
When I say
I have at last
Fallen in love with you.

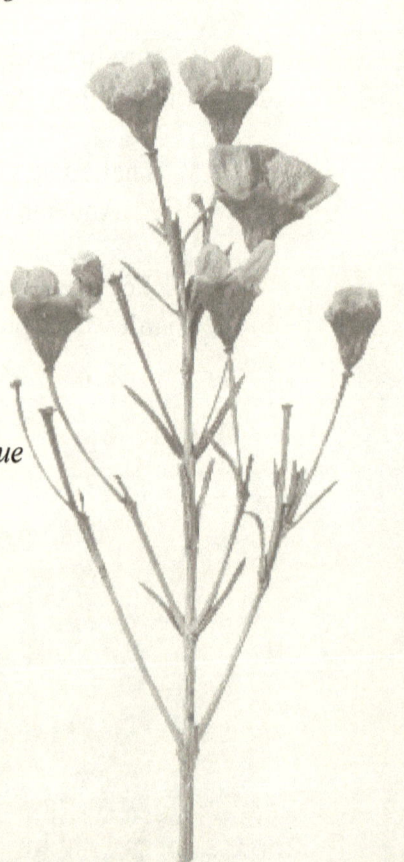

Omelas

(inspired by the city of omelas.)

If we lived in a heaven,
A heaven named omelas

Where every night and day
Our conscience
Haunts us,

Would you walk away
If I were to say
'The tickets are cheap
If you wanna leave,

We can take the next train ride out of here.'

Would you chose to stay

Even if you knew what lies underneath,
Under our feet
Are lies anyway ?

The final song of the origami swans

Good things are gone,
Beautiful memories
Deteriorate with time,

Like origami swans
Build with cheap paper

Unfurling its wings
On blue water dancing

Dancing as it sung
Sung its final swan song.

Famous last words

If your blood still bleeds red
If the flames still burn
still burn the thickets,

In stone
Our fates have long been set

But until then,

There are no gods here
And the living are not done yet.

Lady justice

For she is just;
She is kind
And if you mascaraed
As themis
Dare you not lie-
When did you become def, as well as blind?
Tell me, for how much did they sell.....
Those blinded eyes?

For I have seen children
Starve and die
I see their terror
I see them run and hide

Do you not see their sufferings?
Do you not hear their cries?
Your promises were as hollow
As their lives.

Bitter man,
Angry boy,
The sword is rusted,
Your attempts foiled.
Justice is dead
We lost the fight
The scales grow more and more slanted
As the days go by....

Go home now,
Your life measures to nothing more
Than trouble and toil,

Though they may scream
'Justice is coming'
But I know
She still sees nothing.

Declaration

Sold my soul and a heart of gold
For a shield and a sword
A story untold,
Watch how this unfolds
They waited for cries of despair
To turn into
Cries of war,

Let the blood flow on the battle field
Its been long foretold,
Consider this
As a decleration of war.

No more tears,
No longer kind souls,
Not children anymore.

Nevermore

The ace of my cards
The roots to my home

Whispers into the dark
Nevermore, nevermore

Now I stand nothing more
But a renegade
In exile
Watching all we ever build
Now burn and Burn

Sighing at the sight
At the fading of the light

The twisted knife in my gut
Telling me
It could never be, never be
As it used to be before.....

It could never be, never be
as it use to be before.........

Describe me the night sky –

Stars poke like holes
In the weathred black curtain
The glow of white

Misty gray clouds overhead
Shadowed half the sky
Looming over like puffs of smoke
The bone chilling air

Glowing its brightest it possibly could
In the darkness of this night

As the moon drunk stars
Collapse all for our starsight

Like a painting pictured by the brightest
Brought to life,
Over the suburban Indian sky

Glowing beames of starlight
Danced across the wooden panels
Dancing to the symphony of quite

Through the window they tiptoed
Putting on a show
And all for me and you

If anything is true,
It was my sadness that painted my skies
Their darkest shade of blue

If only I could sing this balled
But alas to whom?
At least the stars keep me company
The night itself shall pass us over soon.....

Ship of thesius drowns

Water beaten ships,
And chipped paint,

Vehemently rocking decks
Over ocean waves

My love, the sea is a beauty
Both
delicate and yet, anhilating

Clandestine, it confides in me
The secrects that lay underneath
For it be a home to many.....

The ocean, I desire and dread
still it calls out to me.

Begging me to drown.

Guns and blows

Your words are like weapons
Each one cuts like knife

Draws blood, as per required
Colossal, each time

Whenever you spit them out in spite
Go around
Destroy everything wonderous
Within your sight.

Im coming back off the edge

I know the very nature of your heart beat
Its music to my ears,

And all this time I've wandered
Wandered all these years

Never knowing I would end up back here

I know you like the back of my palm
I know all your hopes and all your fears

Blue were all my skies
When you first came
To me

Once I have given my all
Screaming out
To the empty surface of the horizon,

Standing Barefoot on the sandy ground,
Breathing in the salt filled air,

In the end I would still leave this, For home again
Home to you.

All gather here

Ocean of glass teardrops
Covered the ballroom floor

After the chandelier drops
After its all over

Broken shards cut me open
Broken shards glimmer and glow

Broken though they be,
Broken aren't they all?

In the ballroom
Where all the broken
Shattered, jagged souls go

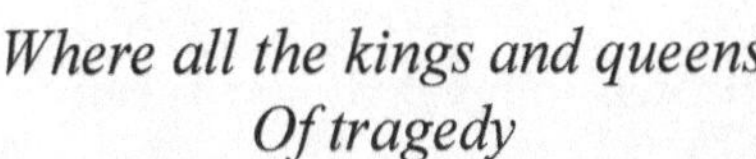

Where all the kings and queens
Of tragedy

With faux jules and shards decorate their thrones

Where jesters dress up as royals
Saying oh what a catlysmic catastrophy!
Such a tragedy!
Laughing at there own failings,
Short-sighted
Just another day at the palace of the lost.

The Feast of the witches

Dear queen mother, Morgana le Fey
Your daughters, your witches stand here today
Another one wronged, another one in pain
Seeking retribution from those who started this game

This is not a plead for help, this is a call to arms
Know- women to women, this is sheer rage.
And on the flesh, the blood of our enemies
tonight
we shall feast again.

We are the new hunters, we reign over this game
All the hellhounds, all the witches
They come together, they sing

Under the moonlight, at the strike of twelve,
Under the shadow of the pitch black dark skies
Dancing to their own songs around the bonfire
Saying'
Oh! Little girl tell me your worst fears,
Bare me your soul
Send my hails to your tormenters,
Let them all know
Bring me a belonging of theirs
And bring me river water cold,
Bring me their blood and bring me some gold
So I may concoct a spell for you or maybe more

The witches of the eastside, ravens of the west
Shapeshifters of the north highs
With the southern sirens, we meet here again
Sisters'
Together we break bread, together we shall have our revenge

A womens rage is more destructive than anything else

And my darlings be assured
They will all burn once were done with them, in the end

Hear the witches cackle, hear their gleeful yells,
Here is where they will bury you
In the garden of your sins

Bury the whole dammed nation itself

Women look out for women, so bring me animal bones,
Preferably the skull, the middle finger,
A spine because they had some nerve

Women watch out for women,
And there is nothing more vicious
Than the scorn of one
And yet they dared to still spite covens
Child,
Tell me how much you want them to suffer?
For this is the feast of the witches

Drink this blood-laced wine and speak her name
With me now 'Morgana le Fey!'
Fierce and enraged
Drunk off this pain
A women is a creature you should not underestimate

Hear the crackeling of the fires, here you meet your end
You too shall lay dead once she is done

Nothing is more dangerous than a womens rage
The fires they now start from our veins,
we don't burn at the stake
Meet the real witches, the witches of the new age

In cloaks of bear skin and fox hide, they sing and dance
Burning traitors heart

On the souls we hunt, apon all our preys
Tonight we feast again.

My blood moon

I had something I've been meaning to ask you

Why does your sun only ever meet my moon
On the most eclipsing of occasions

Why does your light and life
Find me in my darkest times

I only ask of you to answer
How does the blazing nature of your soul
Finds my mellow moon

When every path is blocked
When my soul is bleeding, bruised

Hours turn to days
When I sit here poundering in this daze

They do not like us coming together,
Would I be-what my darkest fears devour?

This will be a fight and not an easy one at that
But if blood is what they desire
Then paint the skies and every river red, I shall

Just for the sake of your sun

Meeting my moon,

Darling I would go to war for you.

And make sure of this,
There will be violence.

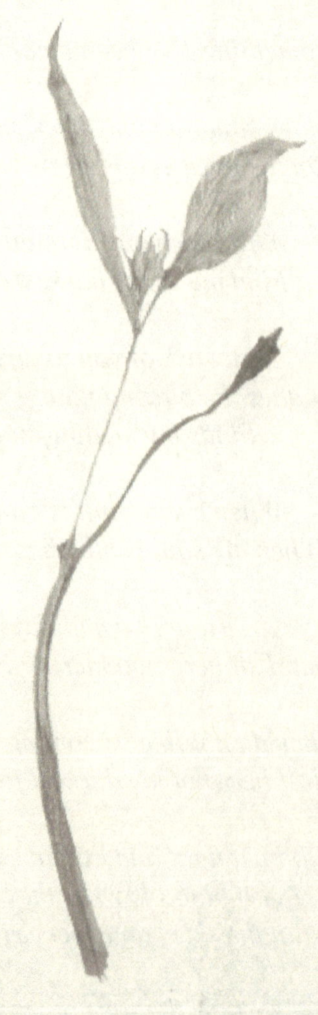

The living too haunt the dead

And everyday I pass by the same street
In my home town
And his widow still weeps over the gravestone
As flowers wither away with time,

Screaming 'when are you coming home!
Oh! When are you coming home?'
Under the willow
She might have stayed there for days
I wouldn't know,

Clanking rung from the bell tower,
And she grived for him, she grived for herself,
She grived for all those who couldn't themselves,
Not anymore no,
No one else came by the gravestone.

Thinking this pain would last her
Till the death of time itself
The widow still grived over the gravestone

But the wind did bend the willow,
Turning the feared fate itself into something more
She sat thinking this pain would be the death of her
But it wasn't though
She moved on

One day she got up and piced together her broken soul
Like a quilt made of love left to her
Both his and her own,
Thus she moved on

And perhaps the soul long past would have asked
For nothing more.

The show at the end of the world

Attention all attendies!
Allow me to pay homage
To the performers
Whose music still reverberates!
And echos! On these halls,

Memories of whom still stalk!
These very halls

Brick by brick
Once the walls come crashing
down
I understand,
We all fear that we just may
Drown,
Underneath the rubble
The same as all those long forgotten

But while we are here
Let us rejuvenate our sprits and celebrate!
For this is the show
At the end of the world!

Drown in nothingness

My sorrows!
Down in the woeful sound of the violin!
The final haunting struck of the bow
At the end of the show.....

Brick by brick the castle falls,
Brick by brick
All we ever build was gone

Even empires fall,
But this?
This was a dynasty gone.

Hold my hand and your head up high
Together we shall face whats been written in the skies
At the end of the world

In my heart I shall hold
The words you once spoke
"We could be immortals if legends never die!"

The tree in our garden is an epiphany

Under the moonlight,
With the star weeping skies

How beautiful would it be?
Resting underneath,

The tree in my garden is an epiphany,

My leaves sway in your breez
Rosegold keys, to my garded, garden gates

Moments passing us by, like gypsies
The keys they slip from my grasp
Im leaving my retreat.....
Leaving your winds to carry me………

The tree in my garden is an epiphany

Flickering lights, the junebugs bring
Leading me out from my darkest times
To back home again, home to you………

The auburn glow, from the hillside
Where our glowing, radiant sun

Died
Now turns violet and blue,
Accented with gold were the grassblades
At the fall of the first ray of sunlight

And while some words
They never took roots,
Some branches
They never grew

All I've ever know and all I ever knew
The elixir of the dewdrops,
The sent of the magnolia's

Darling don't you see?
The tree in our garden is an epiphany

Birds chirped and rejuvinised
And the violet blue skies turned amber
At the morning sunrise

The branches that did not grow
You compensated for……

And everynight I sit underneath
The tree in our garden is our epiphany.

Book Review

Poetry is a doorway to a different world of art. Not only does it irk your imagination but it leaves you with pictures of sites you may have never seen, tastes, smells, all through words on a page. Words can transport you to a different reality and make you experience emotions and ideas you connect with. This particular book of poetry is about growth, about life, death and everything in between. It is about metamorphosis.

Starting from the more simplistic ideas and emotions with poems like 'mother' and 'heart of glass' to poems with more complexity in thought like the 'mortifs of a ship wreck' and 'lady justice' showing the growth from a young mind to an adult with more complicated emotions, the book takes a mystifying journey through the ups and downs of life and human experiences. a tale of growth and metamorphosis. All the turmoil and every small moment of splendour, a true joy to read for someone desiring a somewhat whimsical yet dark journey through a philosophical, revenge filled, bittersweet, homey and nostalgic road, with love and sereneness at its real core.

I wish all the best to Shrshtee Choudhary for all her future endeavours and hope to see more of her writings in the future. I would recommend this book to anyone seeking an escape from reality and seeking to find oneself in a strange and bewildering world. With my best regards to the author.

Anup Rajput
Professor and Head
Publication Division,
NCERT, New Delhi, India

A perfect book to connect you with all the beautiful things in your life. Everything is portrait in a very simple and in an elegant manner. The imagination of the poet/author and the way it is written can easily make you emotional and attached to you beautiful memories. I must say one should surely read this pretty book.

Akash Saraswat
Deputy State Project Director SSA,
Uttarakhand, India

It gives me immense pleasure to see a budding poetess in you; it made me really happy to see your creativity penned down as poems. The poems really touches my heart because they are a great source of experiencing one's thoughts in rhythmic way.

I really wish your stepping stone as a poetess proves to be a successful endeavour and we may see your poems getting recognition globally.

I sincerely hope that you become a source of inspiration for your fellow mates and budding writers.

All the best for your future journey.

Dr. Ritika Dabas
Sr. Lect. SCERT, Delhi

A Feast of Embedded Sensibilities

The poetry book titled "The Wayfaring Strangers" delineated by the vibrant literary personality respected Shrshtee Choudhary is an aesthetic work of far reaching consequences in terms of the ideas presented in it, the evocative nature of the language used, the imaginative soundness of the verses, the philosophical musings so incorporated, the meticulousness so amply shown, the systematic way of its composition, the positive vibe generated by it all along, the artistic perfection brought into fruition by it, the holistic feeling so inducted in its scheme of things and the lucidity so encoded in its delineation. All the poems of this incredible book do maintain a standard of unique sum and substance. These poems also shed light on many aspects of life from A to Z.

The manifold features so innate in this poetry book are:

The Philosophical Constitution of Life

The milk of human kindness does occupy the centre of gravity. This all-encompassing force is the alpha and omega of life itself. The delicate tissue of the human self does contain so many tensions, worries and concerns and it can get into a situation of no return because of the fragile nature of its make-up. The individualism of the postmodern society does whip up so many issues of multiple ways and means. The stability of life is only an illusion and life can get into a shore of downfall at the drop of a hat. The life does have a whole lot buts and ifs inherent in it.

The Implied Thought Processes

Beauty is what beauty does and also it is in the eye of the beholder. Yes, a thing of beauty is a joy forever. But, within the framework of beauty, there is a dark zone waiting in the wings in an obvious fashion. The emotion of love descends down in lightning speed to engulf the human self. The personal understanding is always shrouded in mystery. The expectations are always belied because this world is meant for the highly accomplished. Having a wider vision of life does clinch the spiritual deal at the end of it all.

Timeless Wonder

This world does move along in a trajectory of many ups and downs and ebbs and flows. The game of onupmanship and brinkmanship is played in the open domain of life by recalcitrant elements having no prick of consciousness. The constant bickering goes on with no end in sight. The desertification of the inner self is well discernible when too much attachment to the ways of this world is resorted to. It is better to keep intact the status quo ante. The smooth sailing is at a dead end. The personal inconsistencies and complexes do dominate the internal workings of so many residing in this wider world.

The Faint Glimmer of Hope

The serenity of life can't be discounted. It surges ahead or it does have a way of staging a comeback every now and then. Everything is not lost in the bargain rather things evolve as life goes on. The underlying goodness is undermined by the beastly forces vying for powers and jockeying for positions in this materialistic inclined landscape. This world is a Maya but that truth is conveniently forgotten by human beings. The unsavoury truths are dealt with and the bitter experiences are put in the back burner. Ultimately, the show must go on despite of the many hiccups and glitches, it encounters from many quarters in this turbulent world.

Through this fantastic poetry book, honourable poet Shrshtee Choudhary has notched a significant place for herself in the lexicon of English poetic field. Let her literary endeavours go on unabated in years to come. My best wishes to her all along in her literary journey of explorations and enquiries.

Prof.Cijo Joseph Chennelil.
Head of the English Department.
Kristu Jyoti College.
Changanassery,Kottayam,
Kerala,India.

Poetry is a language of imagination and the vibes of passions. It emenates as a thought in the mind, and gives vent to feelings hitherto supressed, and waiting to be expressed. It is capable of adding pleasure or pain. It's the universal language of the heart, conforming to nature.

Shrshtee Chowdhary, a young and emerging poet, who has quite established herself in previous other works of literature, has come out with a book of poems titled, "THE WAYFARING STRANGERS."

Generally, most poems have to do with melancholy, but Shrshtee's poems go beyond the normal realm, and adds to a constructive and positive approach. Her poems serve as an eye opener to a world that is quite different from the past. She strives to lend a meaning to the situations that confront humanity in today's society. Her poems are a testament of hope and aspirations.

The aspirations of the delights of the heart, for reasons best known only to the poet, are amply portrayed in this book, through her captivating poems.

One can term it as an ardent search of the soul for an euphoric experience.

Perhaps an escapism of the heart from the harsh realities of life? It is through vast imagination that the heart seems to express matters that need redresses, in seeking to make an impact upon the readers, and is quite amply reflected in all its spheres.

The poems vastly reflect deep or serious thoughts, enriched by the use of suitable metaphors, that further go on to reflect the state of the heart and mind, on circumstances confronting a mundane world, thereby seeking to obtain bliss. The work is an overflow of passions and emotions.

In some of her poems, she depicts a feeling of being accountable to the injustices that are inherent in today's society, and she strives to portray a response to the heart's search for a meaningful existence, which is quite evasive in reality. In other words, it can be termed as a silent battle of the heart and soul, against the prevailing conditions in today's world.

Her poems are a mix of various feelings. It encompasses love, compassion, righteousness, and morality, and aims at exhibiting all traits of goodness. For instance, her poem, "Struck by the bow," speaks about the compassion and love of a hunter for a doe that he hunts, then exhibits a feeling of morose for the death of the doe. Similarly, "Paper House" is another such poem that has a mix of different emotions.

Her poetry thus serves as a salve in mitigating the negative attitudes of the mind, and has done ample justice through this work of her's. It truly evokes the hearts and minds of the poetically inclined. A must read for those lovers of modern poetry.

Julian Sujendran,
Poet and critic
Chennai, India

Sometimes, I wonder whether it's the book that gives the pleasure of reading or the one who made our mind nudge and resign from the mundane realms to get ourselves lost. Undisputedly it's the latter, yes, and what if the book is written by a youngster and how one would expect as you go forth reading to be more consuming, the same happened with me as I begin flipping pages, the poems in it strike my heart with their profound imagery and prolific words of spirituality in nature. It's appalling how one as younger as she, could explore the world through the medium of literature to burst out the latent fire to flicker using poetry. I appreciate the way she started right from the word go be it the title of the book " a wayfarers journey" to her dedication implicitly stating her love for "Mother" from where she walked us further to feel respect for "father" and holding the bond of a dear sister, she left the impression of Greek mythology "Apollo's daughter" emotionally touched me with "Struck by the bow" with a tinge of "Hopeless Elixer" the poet showed her side of philosophical and spiritual substance stamped all across the world her poems but what caught my attention is when I turned to page 44 and stumbled upon " Master of illusion" for a moment, I remain silent to experience the jolt left by the "Final celebration", writer succeeded in arranging the array of flavours, yet, so much so imbibing and thought-provoking they are, that, leave the reader to pause for a while and ponder and reflect upon as one read " lady justice" followed by " Declaration" I turned to page no. 42 to watch the "Deadman dancing" that "Killed me slowly" with a feel for "warring species" the young writer transported me to the planet of wizardry with her great imagery as she dished out " feast of witches " till the end of the last page, for me, the book is so engrossing and wanted me to have one more reading. I wish the best for Ms. *Shrshtee Choudhary* for her societal endeavours more and more success, and wish her work be heard not only through her Vocal magic but also among the stalwarts of literature as a starlet to shine forth with an everlasting mark. I give this book 4.6 out of 5 as a rating.

Prasanna Kkumar
Trilingual Poet
Srikakulam
Andhra Pradesh, India

www.ingramcontent.com/pod-product-compliance
Lightning Source LLC
Chambersburg PA
CBHW060449160726
47992CB00003B/1150